To Shirlee
Enjoy the book!
Sandra
a.k.a.
Sue
Harris

# It Doesn't Have To Be Hard
# To Please A Woman

Sue Harris

authorHOUSE®

*AuthorHouse*™
*1663 Liberty Drive*
*Bloomington, IN 47403*
*www.authorhouse.com*
*Phone: 1-800-839-8640*


*©2009 Sue Harris. All Rights Reserved.*

*No part of this book may be reproduced, stored in a retrieval system, or transmitted by any means without the written permission of the author.*

*First published by AuthorHouse 8/13/2009*

*ISBN: 978-1-4490-1097-3 (sc)*




*Printed in the United States of America*
*Bloomington, Indiana*

*This book is printed on acid-free paper.*

# "It Doesn't Have To Be Hard To Please A Woman"

## Preface

The title of this guide book was thought up by a group of friends who were lamenting the sad fact of the poorly educated male in the romance department. Even at the sophisticated age of 50+ most men are clueless in how to successfully court and woo a woman.

We discussed all the commonsense things men could do to make themselves more appealing. On the bottom of the list was sex. Because sex would not even be on the agenda if the man was boorish in behavior. However, if he was thoughtful, kind, attentive and unselfish, the direction of the relationship would be a completely different story.

Therefore the goal of this book is to make both men and women happy, and to enjoy sex as the frosting on the cake in a meaningful relationship.

## Introduction

You would think it is Valentine's Day every day of the year. Romance, or the possibility of romance, is on television and in the news. With all the dating services from Eharmony.com to Match.com, to private match makers, there is a surge in dating. They all offer hope for making a connection and maybe even a long term commitment.

Let us just say that you did get lucky and you have met someone you want to pursue. Now what do you do? Are you prepared? Do you know how to act, to respond and to have good manners? Sorry to say most men have no idea of the above. Men must realize and face the truth that just because you are a man does not mean a woman is going to want you. You have to work on it.

Therefore, the need for this guidebook. It is specifically dedicated to men who want to continue a relationship after the first date. This information will insure a second date and hopefully a mutually pleasant and lasting relationship.

I have observed that most self-help books and articles on dating are directed to the woman. They inform her how to dress and conduct herself. They tell her to be healthy, exercise, and to watch her weight. By the time she has assimilated all this good information she is groomed, fit and charming. If the man thinks all he has to do is show up because he is a man, he is in for a big surprise.

The women of today wants someone who is also charming, attractive, appealing and healthy. She doesn't want to settle. It is time for the man to regroup and rethink his attributes and his short comings.

Women have become picky and cautious about who they date, let alone who they want a relationship with. Women are more independent too. They have probably been married, raised a family and are financially secure. They don't really need a man. Even if they are not financially independent, they don't want to be saddled as a nurse or be with a boring, rude, clueless, fat, conceited man. Most would feel it would be better to be single than to be harnessed with someone so unappealing.

Men might think women are just dying to go out with them but in reality they have to be very special to get a second date. The woman of today does not sit waiting by the phone. She now has caller i.d. and can screen her calls.

Hence the necessity for this primer or guidebook on dating. It is full of commonsense and helpful hints on a variety of subjects.

If someone gives you this book, be glad! Or if it is left out conspicuously, read it and appreciate the opportunity to improve yourself. It will help the poorly prepared man be ready when the right woman comes along.

Before I get into some of the unbelievably stupid things men do, I would like to cover the mere basics of good manners.

- Stand up when you meet a woman.
- Take off your hat when inside.
- Open the car door for her.

- Pull back the chair when she sits down to eat.
- Walk on the street side of the walk way.
- Chew with your mouth closed.
- Use a handkerchief to blow your nose.
- Leave the table when you blow your nose.
- Close the door when you go to the bathroom.
- Don't use a toothpick.
- Don't pick your nose.
- Cover your mouth when you cough.

These are a few of the basics. But the following advice has come from experiences. Women want to share some of the ridiculously irritating behavior that could so easily be improved upon. Remember "It doesn't have to be hard to please a woman."

1. When talking to your date, please look into her eyes and not at her breasts. This is especially true if she is a full figured woman; in which case she is undoubtedly tired of having men gawk at her breasts. Be different and pay attention to her from the neck up, not the neck down.

**<u>Bottom line:</u>** You show your immaturity and lack of sophistication by staring at your date's bust line when you should be concentrating on her mind.

2. If your date has driven over to your house or met you some place it is only thoughtful and polite to call her and see if she has arrived home safely.

**Bottom line:** By calling, it shows you care about her and her safety.

3. A woman does not want to be called "baby". This is not an endearing name. It is a name that can be given to anyone and probably has been. It is not special in any way.

**Bottom line:** It shows you are crass, unimaginative or have a bad memory.

4. When out on a date, do not, I repeat do not look at other women or flirt with the waitress. It might be a natural instinct but believe me it is a complete turnoff to your date who has gone to the trouble to get ready and to be appreciated.

**<u>Bottom line:</u>** Your eyes should only focus on your date.

5. Good hygiene is so important for a future date. Why do stores stock deodorant and soap? Because it makes people smell good. It is a huge turnoff to have a man reach over to give you a hug or a kiss and be knocked out by body odor and stale perspiration.

**<u>Bottom line:</u>** Take a shower and wear deodorant.

6. Dental hygiene is also important. Brushing your teeth, flossing and using mouthwash will make you more desirable as well as healthy.

**Bottom line:**  Sweet smelling breath and clean teeth are more appealing and conducive to a reciprocated kiss.

7. Good grooming is important to being attractive. Make sure your shirts are laundered, your suits clean, ties without stains, shoes polished and in good repair. All these little things add up to a well presented man.

**Bottom line:** Careless, sloppy, disheveled in appearance shows you don't care and that you are probably neglectful in other areas of your life.

8. When you pick up a date get your car washed. Throw out the empty coffee cups, newspapers, dirty rags and cans. Make sure the hubcaps are on. And if you need to get gas do it on your time, not your date's.

**<u>Bottom line:</u>** Even if your car is old it can be clean and odor free.

9. Please don't talk about sex all the time. If you are so pre-occupied by the subject try to develop some other conversational topics and interests. To talk about sex, how often you want it, where you want to do it, gives you the intelligence of an eighth grader. A woman of today likes sex but knows there is more to life and more to talk about.

**<u>Bottom line:</u>** If a man talks about sex all the time, her date might wonder if he can really consummate the act or is he trying to stimulate himself by having his every utterance have a sexual connotation.

10. Believe it or not most women, especially on the first date, do not want to see how turned on you are. Placing your date's hand on your crotch is way too forward and crass.

**Bottom line:** Hold off showing your energetic private part. It is not a turn on.

11. On the above subject, do not come on too strong the first couple of dates. Get to know a woman before you lather her with kisses.

**<u>Bottom line:</u>** Holding off on passionate kissing makes it more desirable and wanted.

12. If you anticipate a night of heavy kissing please don't eat onions or garlic beforehand.

**Bottom line:** Commonsense should prevail that onions give you very bad breath which is a complete turn off and repugnant as well.

13. When making love to your date don't put her through gymnastic routines that only performers in Cirque du Soleil can achieve.

**<u>Bottom line:</u>** Trying to contort your date's body for your sexual gratification is not loving or romantic, especially if she is not flexible. Her moans will not be of pleasure but of pain.

14. When out to dinner please do not tuck the napkin in your shirt. Instead put the napkin on your lap and eat carefully and neatly and hopefully you will not splatter food on yourself. If you do get something on your tie it is preferable than looking like an overgrown baby with bad manners.

**<u>Bottom line:</u>** Now that you are a grown up, the napkin goes on your lap not on your chest.

15. Don't take food off your date's plate, especially before she has even tried it. If she offers, great, but otherwise eat your own.

**Bottom line:** Do not taste food without being asked.

16. Do not come on too strong the first couple of dates. Get to know the woman before you lather her with kisses. Your date will think you are a gentleman if at the end of the date, you ask her permission to kiss her. You make a better impression than the man who lunges in with a wet, slobbery kiss and his tongue down her throat as if searching for the Holy Grail.

**<u>Bottom line:</u>** Your date does not appreciate having her teeth cleaned by your tongue or her throat inspected by it either. Watch out, her gag reflex might be quick.

17. On the subject of making love, the soft touch and caress is a lot more appealing than someone who seems to be kneading bread or pulling taffy. Remember this is a human body you are dealing with, not a mannequin.

**<u>Bottom line:</u>** Velvety touches are much more stimulating than rough, tough manipulation.

18. Most women know what they want to order in a restaurant. Don't order for them without asking what they may want.

**<u>Bottom line:</u>** It is very overbearing to order for your date like she is either a child or a fool. You become a typical male chauvinist.

19. When going to the movies do not ask for senior citizen tickets. If you are silly or stupid enough to admit being a senior, okay, buy one for yourself. (My mother at 80 years old was livid when my father purchased two senior tickets to the movies).

**<u>Bottom line:</u>** To save 75 cents at most, you have shown yourself to be cheap, insensitive and basically stupid.

20. Don't give a woman a nick name that you think is cute or endearing. If she has one, fine, use it, but it isn't up to you to re-name your date.

**<u>Bottom line:</u>** If you want to name something, get a dog.

21. Don't talk about how clever, intelligent, gifted or gorgeous your previous wife or girlfriend was. Why would your date want to hear you extol the virtues of someone else?

**<u>Bottom line:</u>** Keep past wives and girlfriends in the past.

22. Watch your diet, eat healthy and exercise. Men with a pot for a stomach are not attractive and appear unhealthy.

**<u>Bottom line:</u>** Eating healthy and exercising gives you energy and good healthy looks.

23. Don't smoke. Nothing could be more out of fashion than stinky cigarettes. Not only are they unhealthy for you, but your date doesn't want her hair or her clothes to smell of second hand smoke. On top of all that, cigarettes make your breath smell.

**<u>Bottom line:</u>** Stop smoking and you will be better off in a lot of areas.

24. When you start dating don't stay too long to say good-bye. Too much of a good thing is too much.

**Bottom line:** Leave something left to be said next time.

25. After going with a woman for a while don't pressure to move in with her. Leave the tote bag with the razor and comb in the car until asked to spend the night.

**Bottom line:**  It is very presumptuous to start moving in without a clear signal.

26. One of the easiest and cheapest things in the world to do is to really listen to your date. Be sincerely interested in what she has to say and be flattered that she is confiding in you and that she feels she can trust you with her feelings. And above all, do not change the subject when she is talking, especially on a subject dramatically different than what she was talking about.

**Bottom line:** Nothing is more flattering than to have someone listen attentively.

27. One thing that also doesn't cost a penny is a compliment. If your date looks nice, her house is attractive, the flowers are pretty, the dog is cute, just simply tell her so.

**<u>Bottom line:</u>** No monetary investment with a huge positive return.

28. A brilliant thing to do would be to send flowers after a date when you have had a good time.

**Bottom line:** Such a small investment for making a lasting, positive and memorable impression.

29. If you drive a convertible please put the top up when you pick up your date. No doubt she has fixed her hair and make-up to perfection and does not appreciate the wind and dirt swirling around her at 60 plus miles an hour.

**<u>Bottom line:</u>** It is simply selfish and thoughtless to leave the top down when driving your date.

30. If you enjoy driving fast do it alone. Most dates do not appreciate race car driving, and juvenile maneuvers on the road.

**<u>Bottom line:</u>** Your date will not appreciate death defying driving.

31. If you anticipate having sex, for goodness sake bring condoms. It is thoughtful for both of you.

**Bottom line:** If you don't supply the condoms your date won't have sex with you if she is smart.

32. Think twice about taking Viagra. Do you really want an eight hour erection? I doubt if your date would appreciate the fact that your satisfaction level is insatiable. Besides, she can get sore during the process of your latent climax.

**Bottom line:** Just because you are pumped up for an endurance, doesn't mean she is.

33. If you have a date over, some soft music playing is nice. It also fills in the gaps when the conversation may lag.

**Bottom line:** Find some sexy music like Sade, Diana Krall, Alicia Keyes and Frank Sinatra.

34. If you are going to invite your date over, clean up your place. Make the bed, have clean sheets, get the dishes out of the sink, do a little dusting.

**<u>Bottom line:</u>** A dirty house is not romantic.

35. The most basic and telling sign of an impolite and uncultured man is to leave the toilet seat up after you have used the restroom. Leaving it up reminds the next user that you are actually human and have to urinate and that you are thoughtless not to put it down for the next person.

**<u>Bottom line:</u>** Put the toilet seat down.

36. When newly into a relationship don't suggest to your date how she should change her hair style, grow her hair longer or change the color.

**<u>Bottom line:</u>** Compliment her on her hair and appearance.

37. Do not expel gas. You are not with the boys, at a frat house or by yourself. Having gas isn't funny, endearing, cute or romantic. It is rude, inconsiderate and hopelessly juvenile.

**Bottom line:** Leave the room if the problem arises.

38. If you want to bring flowers do not bring just one rose. It would be better not to bring anything than one sad, stale rose from the grocery store being smothered by plastic wrap.

**Bottom line:** Send flowers or bring a bunch. One is cheap and lonely.

39. You might have seen a movie where the romantic lead messes up the woman's hair or runs his fingers messily through it. Trust me this is not a turn on. It is a turn off. All the woman can do is think of the hours it took to get her hair arranged in an attractive style. Even a woman with short, uncomplicated hair doesn't want to end up looking like Alfalfa with her hair standing straight on end.

**<u>Bottom line:</u>** Caress your date's face.

40. Buying lingerie for your girlfriend is actually buying the gift for your self so you get pleasure.

**Bottom line:** If you want to give her a gift give something that she really would like, not just a turn on for you.

41. When you take your date to meet your circle of friends or family, please brief her on the names and your relationship to them. It is really hard for your date to be thrust into a new situation with people she does not know without a briefing.

**<u>Bottom line:</u>** It is only courteous to give your date advance information so she will be at ease and possibly even have fun in the new situation.

42. Try to be knowledgeable on world events, the latest books, movies, etc. To be a good conversationalist and to be interesting is not that hard. Just keep current and express yourself.

**Bottom line:** Try to be interesting and informed.

43. Most women do not want to talk about their age.  If anything, most women are age sensitive.  Why else do they buy creams, whiten their teeth, color their hair, diet and exercise.

**Bottom line:**  Do not ask how old a woman is.

LaVergne, TN USA
09 September 2009
157239LV00001B/27/P